MY FIRST Learn-to

RHYME

workbook

Bat - Cat - Rat

Frog - Bog - Log

Car - Far - Star

Contents

Let's start Rhyming

Dog

Frog

Bog

Cat

Rat

Bat

2

Let's start Rhyming

COLOUR ME!

Star

Car

far

Boat

Tote

Coat

Simple rhymes

COLOUR ME!

Bug   Rhymes with   Hug

What else does Bug and Hug rhyme with?

_____

_____

_____

4

Simple rhymes

COLOUR ME!

COLOUR ME RED

Bed   Rhymes with   Red

What else does Bed and Red rhyme with?

- -

- -

- -

Simple rhymes

Ball
Rhymes with
Crawl

What else does Ball and Crawl rhyme with?

Simple rhymes

COLOUR ME!

Pig   Rhymes with   Dig

What else does Pig and Dig rhyme with?

- -

- -

- -

7

Simple rhymes

COLOUR ME!

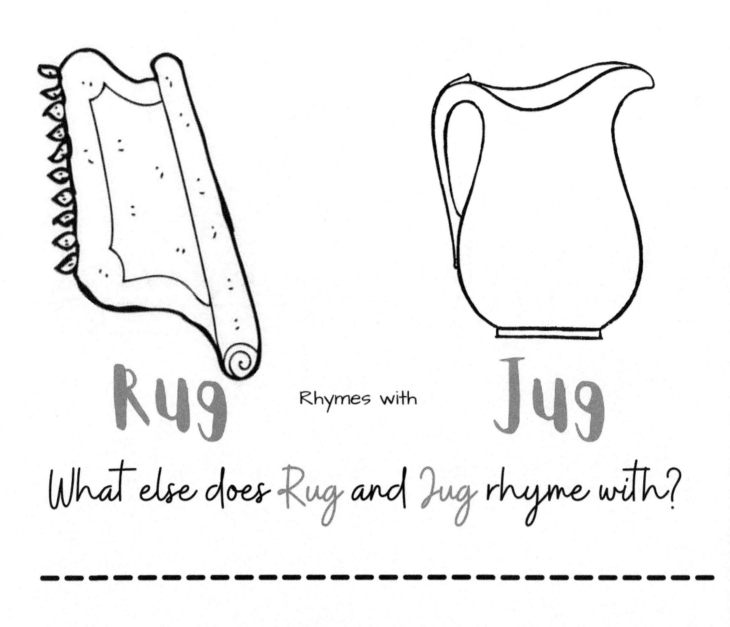

Rug

Rhymes with

Jug

What else does Rug and Jug rhyme with?

- -

- -

- -

Does it rhyme?

Answer Yes or No

Mellow; yellow   **Yes or No**

Bed; Thread   **Yes or No**

Grape; Fake   **Yes or No**

Dog; Hog   **Yes or No**

Beach; Teach   **Yes or No**

The; They   **Yes or No**

Hot; Fought   **Yes or No**

Car; More   **Yes or No**

Them; Hen   **Yes or No**

Does it rhyme?

Answer Yes or No

Fake; Rake	**Yes or No**
Speed; Need	**Yes or No**
They; We	**Yes or No**
All; Forgot	**Yes or No**
Bed; Thread	**Yes or No**
Apple; Hale	**Yes or No**
Cold; Bold	**Yes or No**
More; Core	**Yes or No**
Love; Dove	**Yes or No**

Does it rhyme?

Answer Yes or No Answers

Mellow; yellow   ------------✓------------

Bed; Thread   ------------✓------------

Grape; Fake   ------------✓------------

Dog; Hog   ------------✓------------

Beach; Teach   ------------✓------------

The; They   --------✓--------------

Hot; Fought   --------✓--------------

Car; More   --------✓--------------

Fake; Rake   --------✓------------

Speed; Need   --------✓------------

They; We   ------------------------

All; Forgot   --------✓------------

Bed; Thread   --------✓------------

Apple; Hole   --------✓------------

Cold; Bold   --------✓------------

More; Core   --------✓------------

Love; Dove   --------✓------------

11

Does it rhyme?

Match the words by drawing lines to corresponding rhyming words

Dog   Toy

Boy   Cry

Man   Ball

Call   Fan

Fly   Frog

Does it rhyhne?

Match the words by drawing lines to corresponding rhyming words

New   Stall

Fall   Fine

Girl   Few

Crazy   Lazy

Mine   Twirl

Fill in the blanks

I once knew a man named Fred
He liked to lay in his B_____

Gracie is my dog
She hops aroung like a F_____

I love to go on my boat
All we do is F_____

I went for the ball
But instead I had to C_____

ANSWERS

I once knew a man named Fred
He liked to lay in his Bed

Gracie is my dog
She hops aroung like a Frog

I love to go on my boat
All we do is Float

I went for the ball
But instead I had to Crawl

Fill in the blanks

Today I saw a Rat
And then I saw a C _____
The rat was fast
I knew it wouldn't L _____

I was sitting in a B _____
All I did was float
The water was cold
Not brave enough to be B _____

Fill in the blanks

ANSWERS

Today I saw a Rat
And then I saw a Cat
The rat was fast
I knew it wouldn't Last

I was sitting in a Boat
All I did was float
The water was cold
Not brave enough to be Bold

A rhyme or two!

Finish the rhyme!

I lost my shoe...

GREAT JOB!

We were sitting on a log..

A rhyme or two!

Finish the rhyme!

There was a bear

- -

- -

AWESOME!

We pet a goat

- -

- -

19

write a 3 line poem

Title: _____

- -

- -

- -

Draw your poem

write a 3 line poem

Title: _____

- -

- -

- -

Draw your poem

write a 3 line poem

Title: _____

- -

- -

- -

Draw your poem

write a 3 line poem

Title: _____

- -

- -

- -

Draw your poem

write a 4 line poem

Title: _____

- -

- -

- -

- -

Draw your poem

write a 4 line poem

Title: _____

- -

- -

- -

- -

Draw your poem

Poetry art

Draw something that rhymes with fall

Poetry art

Draw something that rhymes with fall

Poetry art

Draw something that rhymes with fall

Poetry art

Draw something that rhymes with fall

Poetry write and draw

Write and Draw a Poem about nature

Title:
_____

- -

- -

- -

- -

Poetry write and draw

Write and Draw a Poem about nature

Title:
_____

- -

- -

- -

- -

Poetry write and draw

Write and Draw a Poem about nature

Title: _____

- -

- -

- -

- -

Poetry writing

Let's write a longer poem together that rhymes using the keywords below

Title:
_____

- -

- -

- -

- -

- -

- -

- -

- -

Keywords:
Boat
Coat
Float
Bee
Free
See
Me
The
Dog
Fog
Log
Cat
Rat
Mat
Bat

Poetry writing

Let's write a longer poem together that rhymes using the keywords below

Title:

_____

Keywords:
Chase
Face
Base
Maze
Craze
Daze
Haze
Mug
Thug
Rug
Hug
Dig
Rig
Big

Poetry writing

Let's write a longer poem together that rhymes using the keywords below

Title: _____

Keywords:
Bun
Fun
Run
Stun
Pool
Fool
Cool
Rule
Joy
Toy
Boy
Me
The
He
She

Your poems/rhymes

Title: _____

Your poems/rhymes

Title:
_____

Your poems/rhymes

Title:
_____

- -

- -

- -

- -

- -

- -

- -

- -

- -

- -

- -

- -

Your poems/rhymes

Title:

_____

- -

- -

- -

- -

- -

- -

- -

- -

- -

- -

- -

Your poems/rhymes

Title:

_____

- -

- -

- -

- -

- -

- -

- -

- -

- -

- -

- -

Your poems/rhymes

Title:

_____

- -

- -

- -

- -

- -

- -

- -

- -

- -

- -

- -

- -

Your poems/rhymes

Title:
_____

- -

- -

- -

- -

- -

- -

- -

- -

- -

- -

- -

- -

Your poems/rhymes

Title:

_____

- -

- -

- -

- -

- -

- -

- -

- -

- -

- -

- -

- -

Your poems/rhymes

Title:
_____

- -

- -

- -

- -

- -

- -

- -

- -

- -

- -

- -

- -

Colour me rhymes

I once saw a cat

Sitting on my mother's chair

It had ferocious claws

They looked like jaws

The fright wasn't fair

Draw this poem

Colour me rhymes

Eating a piece of toast
I felt I had the most
My sister stepped in and said with a grin
"You're embrassing me, I'm the host"

Draw this poem

Colour me rhymes

My dogs name is Daisy

Sometimes I think she's just lazy

When I take her for a walk

All she does is talk

I'm afraid she might be a crazy

Draw this poem

Freestyle topic poems

Topic: Animal(s)

Freestyle topic poems

Topic: Nature

Freestyle topic poems

Topic: Favourite Food

Printed in Great Britain
by Amazon

34566996R00031